ABOUT THIS BOOK

These poems express faith and trust in the gospel message
and appreciation for the light of God's truth, in the Church
upbringing I had, music playing a major part and in my
teaching career as well. To express ideas verbally and musically
is an important enlightenment of the mind and how life is to be
enjoyed and lived. Trust and caring for each other is as relevant
today as ever.

DEDICATION

I dedicate this book *THE WAY AND THE TRUTH* to my parents. I had a special upbringing which has been my stay throughout my life. They were always my inspiration.

Jayne Marilyn Johns-Davies

THE WAY
AND THE
TRUTH

AUSTIN MACAULEY PUBLISHERS™
LONDON • CAMBRIDGE • NEW YORK • SHARJAH

A CIP catalogue record for this title is available from the British Library.

ISBN 9781398440074 (Paperback)
ISBN 9781398440081 (ePub e-book)

www.austinmacauley.com

First Published 2022
Austin Macauley Publishers Ltd®
1 Canada Square
Canary Wharf
London
E14 5AA

ACKNOWLEDGEMENTS

I acknowledge with grateful thanks Kimberly Melotte BA Hons who has given me friendship, essential computer help, encouragement and support. I so appreciate our combined effort in enabling the production of this book *THE WAY AND THE TRUTH* to go ahead.

CONTENTS

Christmas

TO BE STEADFAST

O to be steadfast in the hope of your coming,
O mighty Redeemer and Saviour of men,
Steadfast in faith, declaring your wonders,
Our rock in a wilderness, our refuge in storm.

Dare we neglect your so great salvation.
Your arm upholding, your love firm and strong,
O to be steadfast with a heart of thanksgiving,
God's manna a feast and the joy of man's soul,
We are but dust and frail in our weakness,
But thou, mighty God, can turn darkness to light,
Great Comforter divine, how can we forget Thee?
Your deliverance, your guidance, your power to save,
From earth's pilgrim way to God's beauteous kingdom,
You're our hope everlasting, the Truth and the Way.

GOD'S WORD IS TRUE

The word of God is true,
And the rock immovable on which we stand,
Through problems of life and troublesome times
We reach out to clasp His firm divine hand.
He keeps our feet from slipping
And leads to a wide wealthy place,
Guiding and guarding by His mercy and grace.

The word of God is true,
His love dispels all fear,
His light is the joy that sparkles with life,
Eyes open to see the warmth of the fire
Of the Holy Spirit, energising, refreshing with God's power,
To change us to the image of our Father above,
Drawing us close to His presence and love
And His peace, which ends all man's distresses and strife.

God's word unshakable stands for all eternity.

FINITE

We are finite,
God is infinite,
A heavenly Father
So compassionate.
When we trust in faith
His heart is moved,
Our sighs, our tears,
His eye sees all.

We are finite,
God is infinite,
A God of love
Who blessings send,
He is the God
Of our salvation,
O trust Him more,
We're His creation.

We are finite,
God is infinite,
The winds and waves
Obey His word,
He is the Captain,
He is victorious,
He is the vine,
True life of all.

COMPLETE FAITH AND TRUST

How dreadful to be left in the cold dungeon of unbelief
When you say, "Come unto me".
How cold and dark and dank is the air,
No light, no hope, all is fear.
No love, no comfort, no food to give strength,
No – one to hear cries of pain.
But, Lord, your glory can break through these walls
To the heart that would turn to your name.
"Come unto me", you say, in love,
For you are the Saviour divine,
You lift us up from the mire and the clay
So our feet walk above and are free.
Your divine sword, your word of truth
The power of the enemy slays,
I come to you, Lord, please lift me up
My human strength always fails.
In mercy lift up to heavenly realms
My complete trust and faith is in you.

THE WARMTH OF KNOWING

The wonder and warmth of knowing you as Saviour,
The wonder and warmth of knowing you as Redeemer,
Truth sparkles in the light of your love.
I stand secure, I rest assured,
Forgiveness heals, I thank you Lord.

The wonder and warmth of knowing that you love me,
The wonder and warmth of knowing that you care,
Great Shepherd divine your pastures are pleasant,
Still waters refresh, you perfume the air.

The wonder and warmth of glimpsing your glory,
The wonder and warmth of your victory over death,
Hope springs eternal in the hearts of your people,
Your pilgrims march forward to your kingdom above.

THE BEAUTY OF JESUS

To see the beauty of Jesus –
Like apple - blossoms on a tree,
The sun filtering its warmth to the earth beneath,
Lord open my eyes this vision to see,
The beauty of Jesus is life to me.

To see the beauty of Jesus –
Like gentle waves lapping the shore,
The soft sound of water speaking its joy,
Speaking to us that our lips employ
Joined praise to our Creator forever more.

To see the beauty of Jesus –
Like the sun's golden glow,
The first morning star and the evening's sunset,
Our Saviour and Dayspring from on high,
Calls us to Him, to be close and draw nigh.

To see the glory of Jesus –
That fills all heaven and earth,
To draw nigh to the Lamb that was slain on the cross,
Shedding His blood to forgive all our sin,
Life eternal giving, to be forever with Him.

To see the beauty of Jesus
Gloriously risen to life,
Death changed and conquered by His power and might,
His light shedding the darkness that blinds the eyes,
His new life strengthens, renews and restores,
His grace changing to beauty ne'er seen before.

Jesus, Zion's perfection of beauty.

FORGIVENESS

Jesus, your blood is the lifeblood of forgiveness for all mankind,
The cleansing power of pardon,
The liberating force to set men free,
The love that always envelopes me.

Love, what greater love, O God
And mercy and compassion
Is brought to man that on the cross
My Saviour died and nought is loss.

Jesus, mighty Saviour of the world,
Jesus, the caring shepherd of my soul,
Jesus you truly are my all in all,
With joy I'll praise and on you call.

Your righteousness, your light, your hope,
Your Spirit enables me to cope
With this barren world's hurts of despair
And with all of my sorrows and my care.

Jesus you tasted death for me,
Jesus your life has set me free,
Jesus your pardon and tender mercy
I'll claim you as King eternally.

My Saviour Lord and coming King,
To you I give my everything,
I kneel before you and adore,
Reveal your glory evermore.

God's blessings are for ever,
His love for eternity,
life of resurrection
Is ours, if we choose to see.

UNTIL YOU RESCUE

The blight of sin pervades,
Its rising force degrades
And drags man away from the light of God's love.
Man blindly tolerates error,
Trembles at the dictate of terror
And clings to the deadness of his idols,
Until O God you rescue.

You come in such great mercy,
To take from the power of the enemy
Poor helpless man and turn him around.
You shed his mind with light,
Clothe in your righteousness so white,
Sin's shackles broken to give liberty,
O God what rescue.

You hear the voice of those that cry,
You want a people that draw nigh,
O God of great compassion, how you rescue.
O that man would hear your voice,
Make your true path his constant choice,
Rejoicing in redemption ever free,
Singing praise, O God you rescued me.

GREAT SIN BEARER

Only Jesus can bear the burden of transgression,
He knows the defilement of sin,
He bore for us this burden
To free us, to wash us clean.

His blood has the cleansing power,
Black sin exchanged for white,
Righteousness pure and glistening
Is ours to walk in His light.

What joy to be found in forgiveness,
What joy to be found in our Lord
Who rescues and saves and redeems us,
The price on that cross fully paid.

Thank you Lord Jesus for giving us
The most priceless gift to man,
You are our great sin bearer,
Our soul's life and eternal healer.

AH! MERCY

How tender, how marvellous is mercy –
How forgiving;
The giving of care to the helpless,
The giving of self to others,
The weak and the defenceless.

O God of strength and salvation,
To the rescue of man you came,
Blind man floundering and hopeless
Only by your strength is saved,
Only by your light can feel mercy,
Then his heart with joy can sing,
How tender, how wonderful your mercy,
Accept the praise I bring.

Is there mercy in lies and deception?
Is there mercy in rejection and pain?
Is there hope in total blackness
For that path is not smooth or plain.
O for skies to open with singing
And for light's rays to glisten with warmth
Showing the path of God's highway
Away from Satan's onslaught.
Here mercy is dressed in such beauty,
God's redeemed are changed by God's love,
Wearing robes of royal riches,
For His mercy ever flows from above.

GOD'S LOVE UNCHANGING

You tasted death for every man,
Salvation great was in God's plan,
Calvary's love still flows to-day
And shows God's holy, righteous way.

Jesus died to conquer sin,
He calls us to remember Him,
To accept His greatest offering,
Calvary's love unchanging.

Man set free is free indeed,
Jesus meets our every need,
In Him I trust, his name revere,
His sovereign will my life to steer.

Majestic Lord, I'll praise and sing
The new song that to me you bring,
The song of deliverance and joy untold,
For the shackles of sin no longer hold.

Iniquity black I'll soar above
With the Holy Spirit's strength and love,
With God's righteousness on I'll walk day by day
And seek His straight path in all my ways.

BLACK BECOMES WHITE

You have picked me up, Lord – black becomes white,
Black sin of destruction that leads to hell's abyss
Becomes changed by your mercy and love that's so warm,
Iron clutches let go and I'm saved from harm.

You have picked me up, Lord, and set my feet
On a firm high rock with a vista so clear,
God's truths glisten like crystal - His presence so sweet,
In the light of His Gospel, I have nothing to fear.

You are coming soon, Lord, for your chosen elect,
Strengthen by grace – keep us watching in prayer,
Working with diligence and serving with care,
Can we ever neglect your salvation so great?
No, great Redeemer, your worth is of weight.

DOWN OR UP

O God, I feel heavy to-day,
No wings to lift me up,
Sorrow and sadness are a slippery downward slope,
The mind thwarted when there is no hope.

O God, I am your child,
And your arms enfold and comfort,
Strengthen me with your strength,
Clothe me with your pure righteousness,
Breathe into me the quickening life of your Spirit
That my whole being will rise by your grace,
Lifted up to bask in the beauty of your holiness,
Not down, but up, in the glory of the heavenlies,
Risen high above the battles of conflict
And the sparks that fly upwards of
Man's mortal contentions,
Up, rejoicing of mercy and deliverance,
Forever in you lifted up.

BE LIKE ONE OF THEM?

Be like one of them? Who?
The godless of this world.
Anxious for gain, a hard bargain drive,
Then we're like one of them.
An offensive remark, we laugh just the same,
Then we're like one of them.

Dare we put our hand to cunning deceit,
Our lips speaking easily a lie,
Do we condone abuse of God's name,
Or abuse of God's sacred day.
A difference must be seen in children of God,
A difference to stand up and speak.
We're different, we cannot be classed the same,
God's armour wearing, His truth declaring,
His new creation the difference making,
To help us not be like them.

IS THERE FAMINE

If there's famine in the land,
Is there famine in our hearts?
Should we not, like Ruth, glean and the Master seek,
And be comforted by the richest owner of the field.

His merciful kindness and insight sincere,
Her needs he met with discernment clear,
A foreign girl, but a diligent worker,
Her trust and faith were in her new master.

With an open-heart Ruth came to find
That this was the place that gave peace of mind,
Protected and sheltered she found refuge sweet,
Benevolence and care from the rich man's feast.

A stranger, she had been taken in,
Love shown, that with gratitude she bowed the knee,
She came to know the God of this land
And to Boaz, her kinsman, she held out her hand.

With an open heart, we too, must seek the Lord,
Be sanctified by faith and feed on His word,
Seek the Great Shepherd who meets every need,
And by grace and joy we sit at His feet.

The Lord calls us to feast and banquet with Him,
We are not outcasts, we are called to come in,
To be as God's chosen, His bride, His elect,
What joy and what privilege to be His select.

Let's seek like Ruth, let's be at Jesus' feet,
Anointed, cleansed, and washed from sin,
Listening with intent to His voice that will guide
Through earth's pilgrimage 'til we land on Canaan's side.

When there the fullness of joy will be ours,
E'en now Heaven's windows send forth its' great showers
Of mercy, compassion and healing divine,
Like Ruth, seek the Saviour, and His great love sublime.

Jesus, the Christ, gave His life, gave His all,
Still calls, "sinner come" my love is for you,
New life I give, eternal and free,
My atonement was for all mankind,
Just simply believe on me.

FIGHT THE GOOD FIGHT

Flawed, marred and imperfect,
Lord melt my heart.
How can I be so arrogant and proud?
When Satan knocks so loud,
And entices and captures as he prowls?
Strong is his jump, powerful in attack,
A master marksman on those he preys.
Lord, mighty God, you know his ways,
He is the prince of death.

But, you the mighty risen Lord,
On Calvary's cross you conquered all,
You smote sin's slavery with your breath,
You set so free that we can soar
To heavenly realms and on you call.
With the shield of faith and the two-edged sword
We fight the good fight, for you are Lord.
Lord of all life and sovereign supreme,
Lord above all loves, on you we lean,
Victorious in the eternities,
Majestic glory beyond all dreams.

THE NAME OF JESUS

What does the name of Jesus mean to us?
Is it the highest name? Is it the sweetest name?
Do our hearts stir within us when we hear this name?
Or talk of all His wondrous ways.

This name is at the core of all our needs,
Like the hub of a wheel, each spike reaching to hold and support
Each spike shining with God's light and warmth,
Mercy and compassion keep the wheel turning with hope eternal,
His truth guides on His direct straight path.

What does the name of Jesus mean to us?
Does it not encompass life of very life –
Does death have the victory when the keys are in His hand?
His name Emmanuel, God given, God with man.

His promises are sure and Amen,
Salvation only through His name,
Our mediator and High Priest on High,
He reaches down to melt our stony hearts,
To cleanse, forgive and make anew,
To make us ready for His perfect paradise.

What does the name of Jesus mean to us?
It is the highest name, it is the sweetest name,
He is our great Redeemer and our friend,
King of Glory, King of Kings, Master and Creator, we bend the knee,
With gratitude may our praises rise to Thee.

GOD'S KEEPING POWER

Jesus, joy of the whole world,
Jesus, balm of my soul,
Jesus, quickening life anew
That heals and makes me whole in you.

Jesus, you are the Gospel's light
Your rays light up the path we tread,
You keep, you hold, you guard and guide,
With eyes looking upward, no fear or dread.

Jesus, Saviour of the cross,
Help me to grasp the price you paid,
You rose to show us your new way,
Keep me by your power I pray.

WHICH SIDE?

To lose and be lost forever
Is to fight on the devil's side,
To wallow in ignorant indifference,
To not know the victory side.
To not care of evil's destruction,
To not feel the blight of its snare,
To not heed God's voice of correction
His love of redeeming care.

His is a wake-up call earnest,
His the changing power of good,
His mercy so great it's enthralling,
His forgiveness through Calvary's cross.
His blood shed to break Satan's enslaving,
His risen life the power over death,
He is the first to lead God's chosen
In eternal victory and glorious array,
On the winning side my Lord and my Saviour,
I shout the battle cry, and follow your way.

ZION'S PERFECTION

Praise wells up with exuberant joy
When hallelujahs our lips employ,
To sing of our soul's eternal delight
The Lord of all heaven's Glory bright.

Jesus the Lamb, the pure Holy one,
Cried on the cross, "It is finished" – it is done,
His sacrifice complete, His sacrifice supreme,
His blood shed for redemption and forgiveness of sin.

Peace and righteousness meet through this act of God divine,
By faith, when we believe, eternal life is yours and mine,
The beauty of holiness is ours and we're set free,
In Jesus there is new life, and in Him true liberty.

Zion's perfection of beauty, no unclean thing can spoil,
The treasure of New Jerusalem, the holiest of all,
The place of joy unspeakable, no sorrow, pain or tears,
Jesus is our all in all, now, and for all eternal years.

LOOK FOR GOOD

Don't look for faults in me, just look for good,
Let's keep our eyes on Jesus as we should,
Let's seek to be like Him
God's holy son in whom no sin.

Where but for mercy would we be,
Where but for compassion full and free,
O to have a heart that melts with tears
For the living God draws near.

O for ears to hear and eyes to see
The beauty of light and truth and purity,
The holiness of righteousness divine
God's enfolding love, by faith, is yours and mine.

Look to the one who says, "Come unto me,"
"All you who are weary, come unto me,"
Christ lifted up draws to Himself all men,
Though all have come short of His glory in heav'n.

Where but for mercy would we be,
Where but for compassion full and free,
O to have a heart that melts with tears
For the living God draws near.

Don't look for faults in me, just look for good,
Let's keep our eyes on Jesus as we should,
Let's seek to be like Him,
God's holy son in whom no sin.

BEAUTY FOR ASHES

Not cast on a rubbish tip of useless worth,
But picked by a hand of tender love and truth,
And kept, the price paid, Calvary's price,
Kept to be polished, displayed and cherished,
Made as a jewel for God's eye to behold,
To be placed in Heaven's glory, if our trust is pure like gold.

Just as a little lamb I bleat with joy
Because I know you, Saviour, King,
Your hands keep me warm and safe,
Your voice comforting, calms, when weak limbs are trembling,
Yet, you're a God of strength, and on your strength we rely,
You keep feet from slipping, you guide with your seeing eye,
Your path the floodlit way of righteousness,
Your truth sparkling like gems,
Your grace as tender as soft rose petals,
Your mercy a fragrance exquisite and rare,
Your beauty so wondrous that nothing can compare.

O God of redemption and salvation sweet,
In humbleness I bow at your Kingly feet,
Please accept my thanksgiving and praises due,
All power and beauty is yours of every hue.

GREAT SHEPHERD

Gazing across the fields I love to see
Sheep grazing in peaceful simplicity,
Their wool soft, like white plump pillows,
Scattered, for our eyes to see.

Your eyes, O Lord, day and night watch and care,
For we are your sheep in your pastures fair,
Jesus, great Shepherd, you love with such love,
Still waters to calm, our bleatings you hear.

Great, great Shepherd of such tender heart,
We hear your voice for we are yours,
You lift us up and carry us through,
When weak, you make strong, and hold close to you.

Within your fold we are safe and secure,
Your fellowship sweet, your air so pure,
Nothing can destroy or tear us apart,
From your healing grace we would never depart.

JAIRUS'S DAUGHTER

Jairus's daughter lay sick on her bed,
Desperately ill, desperately ill,
Jairus, her father, the house he fled,
What could he do? What could he do?

All hope seemed to fade and people wept sore,
Desperately ill, desperately ill,
Could it be she would be no more,
A child to die, a child of twelve.

Jairus, he sought the Lord to find,
To beg Him to come, to beg him to come,
He pushed his way through crowds that thronged,
And pleaded his plight, and pleaded his plight.

Then as he spoke the message came,
Your daughter is dead, your daughter is dead,
Too late to trouble the master to come,
We weep and mourn, we weep and mourn,

But Jesus knows about life and death,
He went to the house, He went to the house,
Saying," Only believe, she shall be made whole,
Have faith in me, have faith in me."

He stretched out his hand, saying, "Maiden arise,"
She rose back to life, she rose back to life,
What wonderful power from our Saviour divine,
We, too, through Him, we, too, through Him
Shall live.

FAITH IN A FATHER'S LOVE

By faith your righteousness turns the enemy to flight,
What a God, so with us, for His the might,
Darkness cannot prevail against His light,
His love, His compassion, His insight.

O, the cords of love that draw,
In His love He hears our supplication
And opens our eyes to see His revelation,
And kindles the faith that is life's very core.

He sees the uniqueness of each of His creation,
Each one of us His child safe and secure,
With a father's loving hand and sweet correction
He guides and guards, His blessings ever sure.

We need a little faith that grows in God's love,
That grows in heavenly grace shed from above,
That we may show God's love to all around us,
For great His love, and in His promises we trust.

JOYFUL TEARS

Help me not to forget Calvary,
The blood that was shed for me,
The Holy Lamb that was slain,
The Holy Son that was given,
Jesus, Lord, and King of Glory.
Still your love is a banner o'er me,
A love which no love surpasses,
A love which dwells within the heart,
Your life and love to me impart,
For your light dispels all darkness,
Your love dispels any fear,
Calvary's gift of forgiveness and love
Melts my heart with joyful tears,
Lord, I look to your coming again,
Then, with you, all saints
Shall eternally reign.

A MELTED HEART

How can my heart not melt within me,
With tears of gratitude?
How can my heart not melt when I see
The light of God's love and warmth for me,
That changes my heart to make like His own,
That changes this very heart of stone.

How can Calvary not move my heart,
When Lord, you gave your life for me,
Died that I might be set free
To walk in your love and liberty,
To keep your ways and walk your path,
My heart filled with your love is all I ask.

CALVARY'S LOVE

You died upon that cross,
You died and took my place,
My sin you bore, my Lord, my God,
That I might live and love embrace.

Love still flows forth from Calvary's Hill,
The place where I must linger still
And kneel with trembling thankful heart
For all that your love and power imparts.

Your resurrected life
Crowns every day with joy and hope,
Sins that held no more have sway,
Your blood has washed my sins away.

Saviour your risen glorious life,
Saviour your risen conquering power,
Saviour your sweet forgiving love
I claim by faith and yours my trust.

EMPTY

An empty glass is empty,
Just as our lives can be,
Unless, as day by day, we scrutinise
Our words and our activity.
O may we drop into that glass
Tiny pearls of kindness,
Pearls that shine with brightness
Exuding care and warmth.
And the more that glass is filled with pearls,
God's love and righteousness
Brings forth the colour of His mercy and His love,
That glass no longer empty
But filled with vibrant life
Extending from a heart that's full,
God's face smiling from above.

A GARDEN

A garden is a private place of beauty,
It is personal, a special place to us,
We tend and care, root out the weeds and briars,
Stand back to admire the flowers that perfume the air.

Is our heart such a garden, unique and fair?
Design of breath-taking colour,
A place of calm, a place of peace
From worries, the place of our release.

Jesus' love dwells in our heart,
From the barren wilderness He gives it water,
Life springs forth from the stony ground,
In his garden beautiful flowers abound.

Do we invite the choice gardener into our heart?
Do we guard it for Him alone?
Do we sit and commune in this special place
Our hearts garden changed by His power and his grace?
Make my heart a beautiful garden that is yours O Lord,
A garden that you will delight to call your own,
A place where you will come and call out my name,
I will hear and my divine Saviour and Gardener claim.

THE KING'S HIGHWAY

The King's highway, the King's highway,
No unclean thing is there,
No unclean thing of hurt or despair,
No sorrow or sadness or sighing.
Look, see and walk in joy and peace,
In the beauty and light of God's highway,
Feet walking on firm and even ground,
No falling, wavering or stumbling.
Eyes seeing the glory of love divine,
No bitter cold shivering or trembling,
Secure and steadfast in the warmth of God's love,
Wearing white robes of righteousness sparkling,
Hearing heavenly music from voices rejoicing
Acclaiming the power of the Lamb that was slain,
His power of forgiveness and cleansing.
No shackles or chains that choke or restrain,
His power the prison doors opening
Setting free to walk on the King's highway,
His purity and truth golden filigree,
The jewels, the crowns, the harps and the sound,
No night to darken the view,
The King of all Kings holds sceptre and sway,
His power and might the light and the way,
His holiness shines, His victory complete,
The redeemed shout the great shout of joy,
No hunger or thirst in this land that lasts,
God's river of life freely flowing,
His way, the King's way, exalt in your heart,
For the King of this highway is coming.

REFLECTION

1.

On the cross He took our name,
All our sins and all our shame,
Shed His blood to cleanse and heal,
Before the throne of Grace I kneel.

Chorus:

His saving and redeeming power,
His loving kindness ever true,
He gave His life that we may live,
In Him restored and made anew.

2.

Three days in the grave he lay,
Fighting all man's enemies to slay,
He crushed them all in victory,
And rose in glorious majesty.

Chorus:

His saving and redeeming power,
His loving kindness ever true,
He gave His life that we may live,
In Him restored and made anew.

3.

What love for us that Jesus died,
The perfect sacrifice He made,
Reconciling man to God
The atoning sacrifice complete.

Chorus:

His saving and redeeming power,

His loving kindness ever true,

He gave His life that we may live,

In Him restored and made anew.

4.

In heaven glorious shouts ring out,

The saints in glory see their King,

He reigns supreme in peace and joy

A banquet is spread for all can come in.

Chorus:

His saving and redeeming power,

His loving kindness ever true,

He gave His life that we may live,

In Him restored and made anew.

THANK YOU LORD

You died for me – Thank you Lord,
You've set me free – Thank you lord,
My spirit rises to heavenly heights
To walk in the King's highway.

Wearing your robes of righteousness white,
Singing the new song of your power and might,
The redeemed on this Highway a glorious sight,
Thank you Lord.

Sin's pernicious decay, its sorrow and tears,
Constantly seeks to mock and to jeer,
But the Lamb that was slain on Golgotha's hill
Purged it away, His blood forgives still.

The price paid in full, the pain of that price,
That cruel death borne to give men new life,
I kneel to remember your mercy so free,
My conquering Saviour of Calvary.

WHOLE AGAIN

Iniquity taken away and sin purged,
How clean am I, how clean?
Your righteousness, O Lord, clothes in white array,
Your glory and your light shines brighter than the day.
May the fire from off the alter of your presence
Touch the very essence of my being,
My thoughts, my very words, my very deeds,
That I may come to the tenderness of your holiness,
The awesome beauty of your purity,
The earthly magnitude of your compassion,
That I may be made whole again,
Healed, and made whole again.

HOLINESS IS BEAUTIFUL

Holiness is beautiful,
Where no spiteful tongue
Or cruel illness is.
Holiness is beautiful,
No rocky paths or bitter winds,
Deceit or lies or spin.
Holiness is beautiful,
No hurt of man
For love comes in,
God's love, redeeming man from sin
To live life in greatest fulness,
In God's fulness of joy,
Nothing marred by imperfection,
No grit in the clay God has moulded,
But, beauty to please and enthral,
And ours, to respond to His call,
To walk His Highway by His mercy and grace,
A jewel to be in His prepared place
Of riches and music and beauty untold,
Of peace and calm, no war to unfold,
God's holiness is beautiful,
How I long for beauty,
God's holiness is beautiful.

NEVER TO BE FORGOTTEN

The one who paid the full atoning price,
Can't forget the torture and the pain
Of dying on that callous wooden cross
And lifted up to die.

His scars cry out as witness and they ever speak,
Slain Lamb of God bore this pain for us,
Can we forget this sacrifice divine?
Can we forget that we are lifted too?

Lifted by God's love that sets us free,
No longer bearing hurts of black sins misery,
And seeing the scars of our glorified Lord,
We kneel with a heart if deepest gratitude.
Remembering.

FAITH

The faith we have is precious,
Simon Peter the Apostle says,
To glory and holiness God calls us,
His promises yea and amen.
Through Christ we escape corruption
And the evil of this world.
Let's stir up our remembrance
And our hearts establish in truth,
Expressing God's divine nature
In brotherly love and good works,
To be fruitful in knowing our Saviour
And the power of our coming King,
Peter witnessed, saw our Lord's majesty
And heard God's heavenly voice,
Take heed, says Peter, and listen,
Make Jesus your heart and soul's choice

HEAVENLY BLISS

Pale shades of grey turn to black
If the truths of God's Holy Word we lack,
Two wrongs never make a right
The true continuance of man's plight,
His prospect a godless black abyss,
And to reject by unbelief his greatest loss,
When the light of God's love he shuns,
The love of those arms outstretched on the cross
Bearing the weight of sin and dross,
Merciless lies and blasphemy.
The one who says , Look I die for you,
I die to redeem and change you anew,
My love forgives,
My righteousness clothes in white array,
My truths heal, my light guides the way,
My purity and holiness the joy of each day,
My compassion and mercy meet with a kiss,
To be a child of God is heavenly bliss.

COMING AGAIN

Jerusalem, Jerusalem,
Centre of faith and hope of resurrection,
Golgotha's hill is reminder stark,
The finger of death points and leaves his mark.
The great I AM came and walked with man
God's ways to show and freedom's plan.
He laid down His life and took to Himself
All of man's burden and dread and loss,
That burden borne for us on Calvary's cross.
Yet risen in victory, in might and in power,
His life He gives, life that death no longer can claim,
For He is very life, Creator and Lord,
Come, believing accept, this Lordship divine
That in love He stoops down, saying "You can be mine"
All is in Jesus, God's Holy Son,
Just believe all His great victory has won,
All over the world His story is told,
Look to Jerusalem, His coming is gold.

THEREFORE STAND FAST

Therefore stand fast,
A phrase of strength and perception,
Therefore stand fast,
For the Lord is coming soon,
Therefore stand fast,
Let no man deceive you
With wiles of evil destruction,
With ways of unrighteous pleasure and
Death their joy.
Blind they fall in their unbelief,
They defy truth in their delusion.
Stand fast,
Do not be shaken in mind or troubled,
God's love is warm protection from fire,
His truth firm ground on which we stand,
In the light of His light we clasp His hand,
For we know Satan is ever the liar.
Stand fast,
Stand fast in redemption bought with a price,
Our pardon sealed by the victory of the cross,
Our Lord and Saviour rose with might and power,
And Satan's day is coming to an end.
Stand fast,
For at Christ's coming, all evil and terror,
And pain and death, will be consumed
By the very brightness of His eternal glory.
Stand fast,
Let's worship and adore.

CHRISTMAS

BETHLEHEM'S BABE

The wonder of Bethlehem's Babe – Jesus,
Came my heart to save,
Came to shed God's love abroad
To all mankind,
Came to turn around
Weakness into strength,
Sorrow into joy,
His praise, not hate, our lips employ.

The wonder of Bethlehem's babe – Jesus,
God stretching forth His love to man
To take the chains of sin away,
Opening the eyes from blind iniquity,
The ears to hear His truth,
Melting the heart by His mercy divine,
His birth proclaimed by heavenly singing,
Men bowed their knee.

A MANGER

Jesus in a manger,
Don't leave Him there a stranger,
He grew a man, the cross He bore,
To give life and peace for evermore.

Jesus in a manger,
Don't leave Him there a stranger,
Kneel with open heart to see
His greatest gift of love is free.

Jesus in a manger,
Don't leave Him there a stranger,
The wise men knelt with gifts of gold,
His, the greatest story ever told.

Jesus in a manger,
Don't leave Him there a stranger,
He rose triumphant from the grave,
His love and power alone can save.

By faith kneel as the wise men did,
By faith accept His blood was shed,
On Calvary's cross He gave His all,
Ever His message may we tell.

Jesus in a manger,
Don't leave Him there a stranger,
Kneel and give thanks, give praises due,
Christ died for me, He died for you.

THE CHRISTMAS GIFT

Jesus is the gift of Christmas,
The precious gift to all mankind,
His love the greatest gift of all,
If we open heart and mind.

To be loved, a present given,
Sets an inward warmth and glow,
The smile of pleasure lights the face,
Gratitude speaks with its hug and embrace.

Treasures of all earth and Heaven are His,
Creator Lord, the giver of life and joy,
Like jewels of every colour and hue,
His word the gift, His promises true.

Do we ever say no to a gift-wrapped parcel,
Then why say no to God's gift of grace?
And why not knee at Bethlehem's manger
To thank God for the gift of His son, our Saviour.

Christmas is the time of greatest hope,
God Himself made visible in flesh,
The heavens opened with song and glorious light,
God's love the incarnate answer to man's sinful plight.

Jesus, our great Redeemer paid the price,
Laid down His life for sinners to be free,
Clothed in His righteousness we're set at liberty,
Made alive unto God for all eternity.

IGNORE CHRISTMAS?

How can we ignore and say that Christmas is not special,
The star was special!
Men followed it – three wise men,
Amazed that it led them till it stopped
To mark the place where God came down to be born as a human babe,
Nothing more.
God became flesh to show Himself with unmistakable revelation,
To show His power of redemption, and His wonderful salvation.

Love came down at Christmas,
To give man back all that he had lost through Adams fall,
To restore to man all that is not of God's light,
To make perfect the beauty that is all of heaven's delight,
Eyes seeing heavy chains of oppression broken free,
Tended and cared for are His chosen,
Fed by His manna their true portion
Nothing more special than trusting in the Great Shepherd's direction.

What is more special?
Jesus came and gave his life,
No man healed like Him and no man spoke like him.
His miracles and wonders for all to know and see,
Like Legion, we too, need to be made perfectly whole,
Like Legion, we need to call to Him who Is the holy son of God
And cry out to the one who has the power,
What could be more special?

Nothing more special than Christ's blood shed at Calvary,
Christ's atoning power to blot out the sins of men,
Blot out, forgive, and make us right,
Presenting us back to the Father as children in His sight,
What could be more special?
To walk His highway of truth, seeing the New Jerusalem's streets of gold,
Bethlehem's babe rose victorious from the grave,
Is there anything more special, more desirous or more precious?
No, Christmas is eternally special.

CHRISTMAS TIME

I love Christmas,
Because Jesus came,
From heaven above,
To show God's love,

I love Christmas,
Because God's love,
Is still the same,
A love we claim in Jesus' name.

God's love a love that never fails,
From December to December,
A faithful, loyal God,
Deep in our hearts let's always remember.

I love Christmas
With a joy that springs eternal,
Hope and peace in God's gift to me,
His glories in heaven, by faith, I'll see.

I love Christmas
The bright lights, the Christmas trees,
The baubles, the glitter, the giggles of glee,
The smiling faces and greetings true,
May the meaning of Christmas sustain all year through.

I love Christmas,
Because of its all-inclusiveness,
No-one should be left out in the cold,
Families travel to be together,
Greetings and gifts to give to each other,
For Christmas is the greatest story ever told.

Jesus is coming again,
He's not the babe to be left at Bethlehem,
God's only son is our Redeemer and friend,
He's coming back to reign,
And His Kingdom will never, ever end. Amen

GOD WITH US

God with us, God revealed
Through His son Jesus Christ,
God with us, God revealed
Through His son Jesus Christ,
What praise and glory are due His name
The highest name forever the same.
God with us, God revealed
God with us, God revealed
Emmanuel, Emmanuel,
Emmanuel.

JESUS THE HIGHEST NAME

Jesus the highest name,
Yet, to a manger came,
The riches of heaven He left above,
Bringing to earth God's greatest love.

Jesus the highest name,
Yet, to a manger came,
Light of the world His life to live,
His perfect peace and joy to give.

Jesus the highest name,
Yet, to a manger came,
Herod's hatred raged forth to kill,
Sin's darkness was not of God's will.

Yet, Jesus gave His life to redeem,
To break the chains that bind and oppress,
His righteousness and purity, so worth of esteem,
Bow down as the wise men bowed and tell
New life He gives, and His praises swell.

JESUS WAS BORN GOD GIVEN

1.

Jesus was born God given,
A new life for man to behold,
A new born babe, God's Holy son,
Given in love as the Angels told.

Refrain:
The glories of Heaven opened,
And Angels the good news sang,
Look, see, stand still and listen,
Christ Jesus the Saviour came,
Open hearts and run toward Him,
Jesus is still the same.

2.

Jesus was born God given,
In love our Redeemer came,
Died that man's sins be forgiven,
Yet he lives forever the same.

Refrain:
The glories of Heaven opened,
And Angels the good news sang,
Look, see, stand still and listen,
Christ Jesus the Saviour came,
Open hearts and run toward Him,
Jesus is still the same.

3

Jesus was born God given,
A light into our dark world,
He bids us come, find peace with Him,
New life eternal He freely gives.

Refrain:
The glories of Heaven opened,
And Angels the good news sang,
Look, see, stand still and listen,
Christ Jesus the Saviour came,
Open hearts and run toward Him,
Jesus is still the same.

4.

Jesus was born God given,
Goodwill to all men bestowed,
A faithful God of such immense love,
All truth and wisdom come from above.

Refrain:
The glories of Heaven opened,
And Angels the good news sang,
Look, see, stand still and listen,
Christ Jesus the Saviour came,
Open hearts and run toward Him,
Jesus is still the same.

CAROLS

Carolling in the winter snow,

Amid the church and village green

Rousing heart and soul in voice

Onwards looking upwards too

Lanterns gleam under silver moon

Sounds uniting the angel's theme

CHRISTMAS DAY

Christ came to redeem

His love is so great

Reach out to him now

In faith before him bow

Salvation free he brings

Turn to him and see

Majestic mercy and might

Angels worship day and night

See his glory and rejoice

Died for our sins

Arose from the grave

You can be reconciled to God through **Jesus**

CHRISTMAS O SPECIAL DAY
(WITH MUSIC)

Christmas, Christmas,
O Special day, O special day,
Jesus came to show the way,
Rejoice, rejoice, our Saviour came,
O glory to His wondrous name.

Christmas, Christmas,
O special day, O special day,
God's love shown to all mankind,
Rejoice, rejoice, our Saviour came,
O glory to His wondrous name.

Christmas, Christmas,
O special day, O special day,
Jesus Saviour we love you,
Rejoice, rejoice, our Saviour came,
O glory to His wondrous name.

CHRISTMAS O SPECIAL DAY

Introduction

Christ-mas Christ-mas O speci-al day O speci-al day

I   I   IV   I   IV   I

Je – sus came to show the way Re – joice Re – joice our

V⁷   I   I   I   I

Savi–our came O glor – y to his wond-rous name

IV   I   IV   Ic   V⁷   I

BABE IN BETHLEHEM
(WITH MUSIC)

1.

The highest name in heaven and earth is Jesus,

The highest name in heaven and earth is Jesus,

He laid His glory by and came with man to dwell,

The babe in Bethlehem God's holy son.

2.

The highest name in heaven and earth is Jesus,

The highest name in heaven and earth is Jesus,

The heavens broke forth in song, the shepherds saw the joy

And heard the music of the message told.

3.

The highest name in heaven and earth is Jesus,

The highest name in heaven and earth is Jesus,

They left their sheep to find the Saviour of mankind,

Bethlem's babe of pure innocence and light.

4.

The highest name in heaven and earth is Jesus,

The highest name in heaven and earth is Jesus,

Gifts were brought from far, the wise men followed that star,

And knelt in reverent adoration.

5.

The highest name in heaven and earth is Jesus,

The highest name in heaven and earth is Jesus,

Let us the message claim, God's peace and love proclaim,

For Jesus is the Saviour of the world, for Jesus is the Saviour
  of the world.

BABE IN BETHLEHEM

The high – est name in Heav'n and Earth is Je-sus; The

IV   V   V⁷   I   V⁷ I

high – est name in Heav'n and Earth is Je – sus; Let

IV   V   V⁷   I   V   I

us the mess – age claim God's peace and love pro-claim for

II   Ic   V   I   VII   VI

Je – sus is the Savi – our of the World; For

IV   V⁷   VI   Ic   V   I

Je – sus is the Savi – our of the World

IV   V⁷   VI   Ic   V   I

CHRISTMAS
(WITH MUSIC)

Christ came to redeem,
His love is so great,
Reach out to Him now,
In faith before Him bow,
Salvation free He brings,
Turn to Him and see,
Majestic mercy and might,
Angels worship day and night,
See His glory and rejoice,
See His glory and rejoice.

Reflective

Andante

Christ came to re-deem His
I   II   V⁷   V⁷

love is so great   Reach out to him now in
I   V   I   I   II   V⁷   V

faith be-fore Him bow   Sal-va-tion free He brings
I   V⁷ IV   I   VI   V   IV   I

Turn to Him and see   maj-es-tic mer-cy and might
IV   V⁷   I   VI   V   VI

An-gels wor-ship day and night   See His glor-y and re-
V⁷   I   I   III   IV

joice   See his glor-y and re-joice   Christ-mas
I   V⁷   I   *Whisper*